Read It! Draw It! Solve It!

PROBLEM SOLVING FOR PRIMARY GRADES

Elizabeth D. Miller

GRADE THREE

Dale Seymour Publications®

Managing Editor: Catherine Anderson
Product Manager: Lois Fowkes
Senior Editor: Jeri Hayes
Project Editor: Julie Carlson
Production/Manufacturing Director: Janet Yearian
Senior Production Coordinator: Alan Noyes
Composition: Carole Lawson
Design Manager: Jeff Kelly
Cover Design: Alison Jewett-Furlo / Square Moon Productions
Cover Illustration: Stan Tusan / Square Moon Productions
Text Design: Square Moon Productions

ISBN 1-57232-436-8
Printed in the United States of America
11 12 13 14 15   10 09 08 07 06

Dale
Seymour
Publications

Pearson Learning Group

1-800-321-3106
www.pearsonlearning.com

Why This Program Was Created

Read It! Draw It! Solve It! is a unique problem-solving program designed for children from reading readiness through third grade. It was created to increase young children's understanding of mathematical concepts through direct visual involvement. For each problem in the program, students will demonstrate their understanding of the concept by creating a drawing before providing the answer.

Students who use this program become confident in their reasoning abilities and are able to communicate easily their understanding of mathematics. When young children work with illustrations they have made rather than abstract symbols, they learn to think of mathematics as problem solving rather than rote learning. They learn to reason rather than simply react, and they develop a better understanding of what they are doing. They also learn to read carefully because they know that they will have to demonstrate their understanding with a drawing.

Students love the open-endedness of the problems. The program encourages creativity in thought and expression, and it celebrates diversity. No two drawings will ever be the same, and many of the problems lend themselves to a variety of solutions.

Moreover, when students illustrate problems, the teacher gets a better understanding of their thought processes. If an answer is incorrect, it is usually easy to tell from the child's drawing where the student went wrong. Given the problem, "Nine people have come to the dance. Can everyone have a partner?" one boy made a picture of nine happy people in a row and answered "Yes." He had read the question as, "Can everyone have a party?" When his teacher helped him to read the problem correctly, he altered his illustration and answered "no."

How to Use This Book

Each book contains 180 problems, one for each day of the school year. The routine is the same throughout the program, although at the beginning of the year you will want to be sure to follow the activity with a discussion period to be sure any questions are answered fully.

Your task is simply to distribute the daily problem to the class and read it aloud if necessary. Students decide on the essential elements, make appropriate illustrations, and only then go on to provide solutions. Be sure they know that they are to draw the picture *first*.

Samples of Student Work _____

by Meghan Williams

The triplets each have 5 balloons.

Jake has 6 more balloons than the triplets have.

Tom has 4 fewer balloons than Jake has.

Patsy has 1 more than Tom has.

Walter has 5 fewer than Patsy has.

How many balloons in all? ___

by Stephen Yorzinski

Make a picture of nine zoo animals.

$\frac{1}{3}$ of them can fly.

$\frac{1}{3}$ of them can swim.

$\frac{1}{3}$ of them have legs.

You may want to use this program as it was set up—one problem a day—or you may want to pick and choose problems according to the needs of your students and how they fit into your other curriculum areas. Note, however, that the problems increase in reading and mathematical difficulty over the course of the year.

Read It! Draw It! Solve It! can be integrated with any math or reading program. A blank template is provided for you on page ix to make up special problems for your class that incorporate specific information your students are learning.

Also offered in this set is an animal themes program with 45 problems each for kindergarten through third grade. These exercises require students to demonstrate understanding of animal attributes as well as math concepts, and provide an intriguing supplement to animal studies units that you may be doing at any of these grade levels.

What Your Students Will Learn

The format is the same as for the first- and second-grade levels. At the third-grade level, however, problems are especially varied. This was done specifically so students will treat each problem as a unique entity and think for themselves what is needed to solve that particular problem. Instead of a unit on measurement followed by a unit on multiplication, for example, students will encounter a fraction problem on one page, a measurement problem on the next, and so on. Some concepts that students will be asked to illustrate at this level are:

■ alternate forms of expressing whole numbers

■ multiplication and division of single-digit whole numbers to 100

■ addition and subtraction of one- and two-digit numbers with regrouping

■ estimating

■ getting information from graphs and charts

■ creating graphs and charts

Most students will be fluent readers by the third grade, and will be able to work independently most of the time. For example, the teacher may assign the problem for day 1 as independent work:

> Draw the following shapes: a red square, an orange
> square, a yellow square, a green square, and a red circle.
> Then draw the three shapes that would come next.

Even at the third-grade level you will want to be careful not take vocabulary comprehension for granted. Review each page before presenting it to the class, and be sure to go over vocabulary which may be difficult. The problem on day 9, for example, requires comprehension of graphing, as well as understanding the words *more, less, most, least*. It is a good idea to do this problem as a whole group activity.

Equivalence is another difficult concept for many students. In the problem on day 84, they are asked to interpret:

> Anandi buys 12 fish and gives half to Paul and half to James.

and:

> What would we need to do to get an equal number of fish in all three tanks?

There should be whole group discussion of the words *equal* and *half* before the students begin.

The following chart lists the thirty math concepts that appear on third-grade mastery tests, with references to the pages in this book that provide practice problems for those concepts.

MATH CONCEPTS FOR THIRD GRADE MASTERY	PAGES WITH PRACTICE PROBLEMS
patterns	1, 2, 7, 13, 21, 38, 69
expanded notation	6, 12, 43, 51, 134, 169
regrouping	70
fractions	10, 17, 28, 30, 44, 65, 66, 68, 109
multiplication and division–arrays	122, 129, 135, 140, 142, 147, 151, 156, 159
addition and subtraction to 18	37, 52, 56, 60, 64, 70, 85, 138
addition and subtraction of 2-digit #s without regrouping	101, 108
addition and subtraction of 2-digit #s with regrouping	83, 117
multiply and divide by 2, 5, 10	8, 14, 27, 48, 49, 86, 90, 92, 115, 125, 129
order and magnitude	9, 15, 33, 95, 97
more/less	53, 63, 121, 130, 133, 160
rounding	128
estimating	150
matrix or array	4, 11, 18, 25, 47, 50, 54, 57, 61, 73, 76, 80
information from graphs and charts	20, 58, 113, 118, 144, 148, 150, 173, 178
conclusions from graphs and charts	55, 62, 77, 112, 168, 171
create graphs and charts	26, 99, 107, 116, 124, 126, 153, 160, 164, 166, 176, 179, 180
write story problems	16, 19, 24, 31, 41, 59, 74, 81, 93, 111, 120, 123, 131, 139
identify appropriate operation	142, 174, 177
simple story problems	29, 32, 84
elapsed time	82, 155, 157, 165
identifying needed information	88, 145, 154
equivalence	32, 71, 75, 78
measuring lengths	35, 91, 132, 143, 158, 161, 162, 163, 167, 170, 175
customary and metric measures	39, 45, 46, 79, 106, 114, 170, 172, 175
estimate length and area	96, 103, 118
telling time	89, 94, 146, 149
money	22, 40, 87, 89, 101, 150, 160
geometric shapes	3, 5, 23, 34, 36, 42, 67, 72, 91, 98, 100, 102, 104, 105, 110, 119, 126, 127, 136, 137, 141, 152

The program lends itself to all kinds of grouping. Whole class instruction is appropriate on some days, whereas on other days students may work in pairs, small groups, or independently. The format will vary from day to day, from student to student, and even from class to class. Some classes are ready for independent work before others are.

At the same time, it is routine that builds confidence. Every day there is a problem that must be read and illustrated—an intimidating idea, perhaps, at the beginning of the year, but reassuring later on. Children who were afraid to try in September are, by February, smiling, saying "I get it," and settling down to do the work.

The students also gain confidence when they are encouraged to be proud of their illustrations. Children are often pleased with their own work, and teachers and parents can build the students' confidence even further by collecting and displaying samples on bulletin boards and refrigerators.

Analyzing delightful illustrations is a lot more fun for a teacher than simply correcting papers. More important, the analysis helps the teacher to better understand individual thought processes, and then to provide appropriate encouragement and assistance. The better a teacher understands each student, the higher will be student success rate.

Moreover, instead of "training" students in specific strategies, this program educates young people to discover what it takes to solve any kind of problem. Because of this approach, students who have tried this approach are not intimidated when confronted with novel situations. They learn to look for more than one way to solve a problem—and sometimes, for more than one answer. Perhaps the most exciting aspect of this program is that as students develop confidence in their reasoning abilities, they take this confidence with them into other areas of the curriculum.

Blank Template

Use the template on the next page to provide your students with special problems that pertain to the work they are doing.

Draw the following shapes:

a red square, an orange square, a yellow square, a green square, and a red circle

Then draw the three shapes that would come next in the pattern.

(blank box for drawing)

Make a row of 30 flowers. The first flower and every other one after that one are red. The rest of the flowers are yellow.

What color is the 12th flower? _____

What color is the 27th flower? _____

What color are the odd numbers? _____

What color are the even numbers? _____

Make a design using four circles, two rectangles, three triangles, and one square.

Make pictures of:

a model of the earth

a stop sign

a dinner plate

a clock

Which one doesn't belong? _____

Why?

_____

_____

_____

Make pictures of 15 shapes.

$\frac{1}{5}$ of the shapes are circles

$\frac{2}{5}$ of the shapes are rectangles

$\frac{1}{5}$ are triangles

The rest are squares.

How many shapes are rectangles? _____

How many shapes are squares? _____

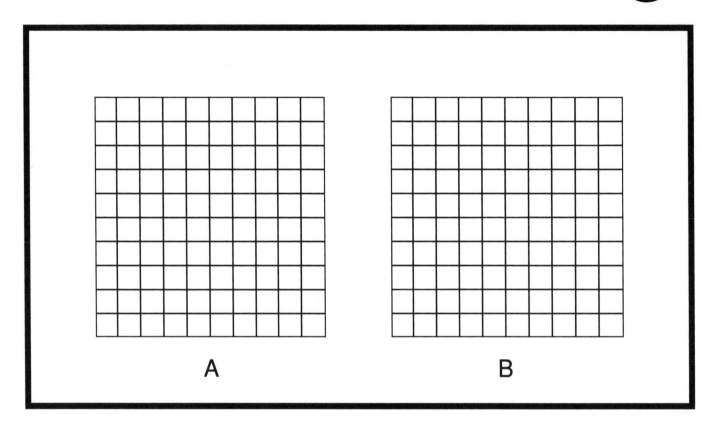

Color in 34 squares on A.

Color in 25 squares on B.

How many squares did you color in all? _____

How many rows of ten? _____

How many single squares? _____

Draw pictures of: How many legs?

a bird

_____ legs

a cat

_____ legs

an insect

_____ legs

Make a picture of an animal that might come next in the number pattern.

_____ legs

There are five players on a basketball team.

How many shirts do we need for four teams? _____

How many shoes? _____

Jie-lu	
Ben	
Carol	
Juan	
Ellen	

Make pictures of differently colored crayons next to each name.

Make up a story to go with the graph, using the words MORE, LESS, MOST, and LEAST.

_____

_____

_____

_____

_____

Make a picture of eight houses.

Color $\frac{1}{2}$ of the houses red.

Color $\frac{1}{4}$ of the houses yellow.

Color $\frac{1}{4}$ of the houses blue.

Name _____

Make pictures of:

    a bat

    a cat

    a bee

    a bluebird

Which one doesn't belong? _____

Why?

_____

_____

_____

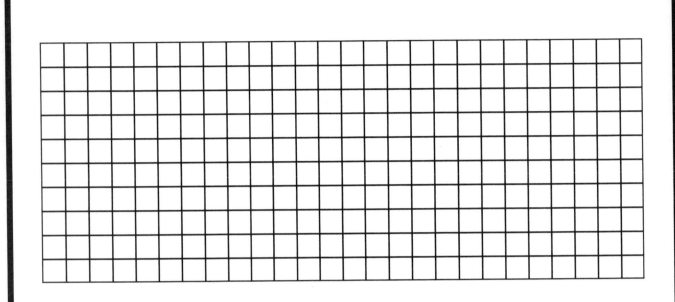

Color seven rows of ten blue.

Color six single squares red.

How many squares have you colored? _____

How many more would you need to color to show 85?

_____ rows of ten

_____ squares

Make a number line from 0 to 30.

Starting with 10, put a blue rectangle around every tenth number.

Starting with 5, put a red square around every fifth number.

Here are ten children. Each child is pulling a wagon.

There are five blocks in each wagon.

Each child holds three kites.

How many blocks? _____

How many kites? _____

The students in our class discussed their favorite foods. We chose 6 kinds of food and voted for the ones we liked the best. There are 25 people in our class. Make up a chart to show how you think we might have voted. Write about it using the words MORE and FEWER.

_____

_____

_____

_____

_____

Write a story to go with this number sentence. Make a picture to match. Then provide the answer.

$$8 + 7 = \underline{\quad\quad}$$

_____

_____

_____

_____

_____

_____

Make pictures of the following shapes:

 a triangle divided in half
 a circle divided into quarters
 a rectangle divided into fifths
 a square divided into thirds

Make pictures of:

    a cow
    a lion
    a goat
    an owl

Which one doesn't belong? _____

Why?

_____

_____

_____

                    READ IT! DRAW IT! SOLVE IT! • GRADE 3

Write a story to go with this number sentence. Make a picture to match. Then provide the answer.

$$12 - 8 = \underline{\quad}$$

_____

_____

_____

_____

_____

_____

	orange	red	green	blue	white	purple	yellow
Dan							
Carla							
Ken							
Angela							

Create a story to go with this graph. Fill in the graph with numbers after you have written your story.

_____

_____

_____

_____

_____

_____

Make a number line from 25 to 0.

Starting with 25, put a purple dot under every other number.

Starting with 24, put a purple dot over every other number.

Tulips cost 20¢, daisies 5¢, daffodils 10¢, roses $1.00, and lilacs 50¢. Arrange the flowers so that the least expensive ones will be on the left-hand side, and the most expensive ones on the right-hand side.

Becky has $1.00. How many of each flower can she buy?

tulips ____

daisies ____

daffodils ____

roses ____

lilacs ____

Make a picture of a square.

Divide it into quarters.

Color the top left-hand quarter blue.

Color the top right-hand quarter red.

Color the bottom left-hand corner orange.

Color the bottom right-hand quarter purple.

Write a story to go with this number sentence. Make a picture to match. Then provide the answer.

$$7 - \underline{\hspace{1cm}} = 4$$

_____

_____

_____

_____

_____

_____

Make pictures of:

    a skunk
    a zebra
    a robin
    a penguin

Which one doesn't belong?

Why?

_____

_____

_____

_____

dogs					
cats					
birds					
horses					
gerbils					
fish					

Write a story about a pet show.

Fill in the graph and write about what you learn from it.

_____

_____

_____

_____

_____

_____

Forty carrot sticks are to be divided equally among five children.

How many would each child get? _____

After each child eats three carrot sticks, how many will be

left? _____

Mom wants to save five carrot sticks. How many must each

child give up? _____

This is half of a whole shape.

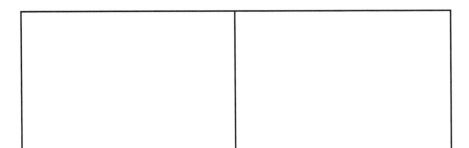

Make a picture of the whole shape in the box above.

Color $\frac{1}{4}$ red, $\frac{1}{4}$ yellow, and the rest blue.

How much of the shape is blue? _____

Kim, Bud, and Sam each have a herd of cows. Kim has two black cows, four brown cows, and three red cows. Bud has three black cows, one brown cow, and four red cows. Sam has five black cows, three brown cows, and two red cows.

How many cows does each person have?

Kim _____

Ben _____

Sam _____

How many cows in all? _____

Are the herds equal? _____

How can we make them equal? _____

_____

This is $\frac{1}{2}$ of a whole shape.

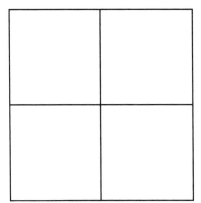

Make a picture of the whole shape in the box above.

Color $\frac{1}{8}$ red, $\frac{1}{8}$ orange, $\frac{1}{2}$ yellow, $\frac{1}{4}$ green.

Write a story to go with this number sentence. Make a picture
to match. Then provide the answer.

$$9 - \underline{\hspace{1cm}} = 14$$

_____

_____

_____

_____

_____

┌───┐
│   │
│   │
│   │
│   │
│   │
│   │
│   │
│   │
│   │
│   │
└───┘

We are playing soccer. The red team has three third-graders
and six fourth-graders. The blue team has seven third-graders
and four fourth-graders.

Are the teams equal? _____

How can we make them equal?

_____

_____

_____

_____

_____

[blank box]

We had a contest to see who could read the most books.

Barbara read four books on Monday, six on Tuesday, three on Wednesday, one on Thursday, and seven on Friday.

Greg read five on Monday, one on Tuesday, two on Wednesday, six on Thursday, and eight on Friday.

Tyrone read three on Monday, two on Tuesday, four on Wednesday, and six on Friday.

Anat read seven on Monday, two on Tuesday, eight on Wednesday, one on Thursday, and one on Friday.

Who read the most? _____

Who read the least? _____

On which day were the most books read? _____

Draw the following shapes:

    a blue square

    a square divided in half with the left half colored blue

    a square divided into quarters with the top left-hand quarter
       colored blue

    a square divided into quarters with the top right-hand
       quarter colored blue

    a red circle

Then draw the three shapes that would come next in the pattern.

Make pictures of things you would use to measure:

a piece of paper

milk

a sandbox

minutes

potatoes

weeks

how much
you weigh

Create a design with one square, one rectangle, two circles, and two triangles.

Make the design symmetrical.

The first-graders have three kickballs, two footballs, and four baseballs. The second-graders have three kickballs, three footballs, and five baseballs. The third-graders have two kickballs, four footballs, and six baseballs. The fourth-graders have one kickball, five footballs, and seven baseballs. How many of each kind of ball are there?

kickballs _____

footballs _____

baseballs _____

How many balls in each grade?

first _____   third _____

second _____   fourth _____

Make a number line from 30 to 0.

Starting with 29, put a blue dot over every seventh number.
Starting with 28, put a green dot under every third number.

Draw a square 2 inches high.
Draw a square 2 centimeters high.

Color the bigger one yellow.
Color the smaller one green.

[drawing box]

Sylvia has one nickel and three pennies. Talia has two nickels. Jie-lu has one nickel and four pennies. Carol has two nickels and two pennies. Juan has three nickels and one penny. Make a chart and show pictures of the coins.

How many nickels are there? _____

How many pennies are there? _____

How much money does each person have?

Sylvia _____

Talia _____

Jie-lu _____

Carol _____

Juan _____

(blank box for drawing)

Write a story to go with this number sentence. Make a picture to match. Then provide the answer.

$$\underline{\hphantom{000}} - 5 = 4$$

_____

_____

_____

_____

_____

_____

Create a design with one circle, one triangle, two squares,
and two rectangles.

Make the design symmetrical.

[empty drawing box]

There are ten grapes in each bunch.

Barbara has three bunches of grapes, two cherries, and three blueberries. José has three bunches of grapes, nine strawberries, and eight raspberries. Sally has three bunches of grapes, eight cherries, four blueberries, and four strawberries. Jomel has four bunches of grapes, nine cherries, and nine blueberries.

Divide the drawing box into four parts. In one part, draw Barbara's fruits. In another part, draw José's fruits. In the third part, draw Sally's fruits. And in the last part, draw Jomel's fruits.

How many fruits does each child have?

Barbara _____   Sally _____

José _____   Jomel _____

Name _____

There are 36 kites in the air. $\frac{1}{6}$ of them are red. $\frac{2}{6}$ of them are orange. The rest of them are yellow.

What part of the group is yellow? _____

Draw a rectangle 4 cm long and 2 cm high.

Draw a rectangle 4" long and 2" high.

Color the bigger one blue and the smaller one red.

Name _____

```



```

Here is a group of trees. The pine tree is 10' tall. The cherry tree is 2'. The orange tree is 4'. The palm tree is 9'. The apple tree is 5'. Make pictures of each. Circle the one that is bigger than the orange tree and smaller than the palm tree.

Make pictures of a tomato, a blue jay, the sun, a beet, a banana, a lake, a daffodil, a stop sign, and the sky. Put together the things that go together. Write why they go together.

_____

_____

_____

_____

_____

[blank box]

Here are three girls and five boys. Each child has ten balloons.

How many balloons do the girls have? _____

How many balloons do the boys have? _____

There are _____ balloons in all.

If each child loses two balloons, how many balloons will be

left? _____

[blank box]

Seven people are standing with their right hands in the air and their left hands hidden behind their backs.

How many fingers do we see? ____

How many legs? ____

Divide the drawing box into thirds. You are going to draw 15 objects in all. Put an equal number of objects in each part.

In one part put things made out of metal.

In one part put things made out of wood.

In one part put things made out of paper.

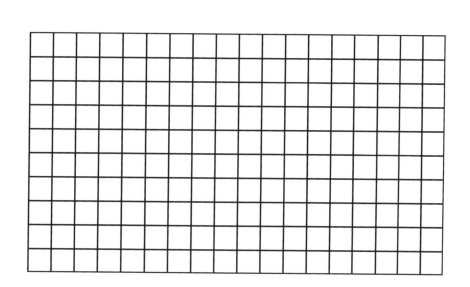

Color nine rows of ten blue.

Color six squares red.

How many squares have you colored in? _____

How many would you have to take away to have 64 left?

_____ squares

_____ rows of ten

(empty box for drawing)

The teacher put three stars on every perfect paper. William got six stars. Zach got nine more stars than William. Teddy got three more stars than Zach. Vicki got half as many stars as Teddy. How many perfect papers did each one have?

William _____

Zach _____

Teddy _____

Vicki _____

```
┌─────────────────────────────────────────────────────────┐
│                                                           │
│                                                           │
│                                                           │
│                                                           │
│                                                           │
│                                                           │
│                                                           │
│                                                           │
│                                                           │
│                                                           │
│                                                           │
│                                                           │
└─────────────────────────────────────────────────────────┘
```

Frank planted five tomato plants and seven lettuce plants.
Giovanna planted eight tomato plants and six lettuce plants.

Who has more plants? _____

How many more? _____

How many tomato plants are there? _____

How many lettuce plants are there? _____

Make a picture of each of these birds, putting together those
that belong together.

   a penguin, a swan, a robin, a duck, an eagle, a canary, a
     goose, and a parrot

Write why they belong together.

_____

_____

_____

_____

_____

       READ IT! DRAW IT! SOLVE IT! • GRADE 3

Beth								
Edward								
Andy								
Carol								
Dave								
	1	2	3	4	5	6	7	8

Write a story about how many hours each of these children played outside. Then fill in the graph.

_____

_____

_____

_____

_____

_____

_____

The blue team has six boys and seven girls.

The red team has nine boys and three girls.

How many people on the blue team? ____

How many people on the red team? ____

How many boys in all? ____

How many girls in all? ____

Make pictures of these different kinds of food, putting together
the things that go together.

   corn, onions, beets, broccoli, lettuce, potatoes, carrots,
      string beans

Write why they go together.

_____

_____

_____

_____

_____

	girls	boys
1st grade	23	31
2nd grade	34	45
3rd grade	46	33
4th grade	37	42

How many girls in all? _____

How many boys in all? _____

How many students in 1st grade? _____

    in 2nd grade? _____

    in 3rd grade? _____

    in 4th grade? _____

Write a story to go with this number sentence.

Make a drawing to match. Then provide the answer.

$$5 \times 7 = \_\_\_\_$$

_____

_____

_____

_____

_____

_____

The brown hen laid 12 eggs. Seven of them have hatched.

The red hen laid 13 eggs. Four of them have hatched.

How many chicks in all? _____

How many eggs are left? _____

Make a picture of these things. Put together things that go together.

    a train, a hot air balloon, a sailboat, a helicopter,
      a school bus, a flying carpet

Why does each group go together?

_____

_____

_____

_____

How are they all alike?

_____

Pat								
Leo								
May								
Pedro								
Nina								

Pat has been on a plane seven times. Leo has been four times. May has been eight times. Pedro has been six times. Nina has been three times.

Fill in the chart.

Who has gone the least number of times? _____

Who has gone more times than Nina and fewer times than

May? _____

Joan has read six books.

Karen has read one more book than Joan has read.

Hiro has read two fewer books than Joan has read.

Dagmar has read twice as many books as Hiro has read.

Doña has read five fewer books than Dagmar has read.

Who has read the most books? _____

Who has read the fewest books? _____

The parking lot holds sixteen cars. There are four empty spaces.

How many cars are in the lot? _____

Four of the cars are red. There are as many blue cars as red cars. The rest of the cars are green.

How many cars are green? _____

[blank box]

Draw pictures of 12 trees.

$\frac{1}{2}$ of them are apple trees.

$\frac{1}{4}$ of them are pine trees.

The rest are orange trees.

How many of the trees are orange trees? _____

How many pine trees are there? _____

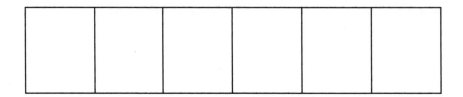

Color $\frac{1}{2}$ of this shape red, $\frac{1}{6}$ of the shape blue, and $\frac{1}{6}$ of the shape yellow.

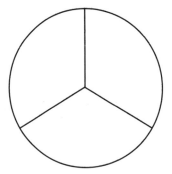

Color $\frac{1}{3}$ of this shape purple, $\frac{1}{3}$ of the shape yellow, and $\frac{1}{3}$ of the shape black.

Color $\frac{1}{5}$ of this shape blue, $\frac{3}{5}$ of the shape yellow, and $\frac{1}{5}$ of the shape green.

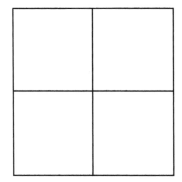

Color $\frac{1}{4}$ of this shape red, $\frac{1}{4}$ of the shape yellow, and $\frac{1}{2}$ of the shape green.

READ IT! DRAW IT! SOLVE IT! • GRADE 3

Copyright© Dale Seymour Publications®

Create a design with two squares, three rectangles, three circles, and four triangles.

Make the design symmetrical.

Make a picture of nine zoo animals.

$\frac{1}{3}$ of them can fly.

$\frac{1}{3}$ of them can swim.

$\frac{1}{3}$ of them have four legs.

Draw zoo animals in a line. Starting with the second animal, every other one is a meat eater. Starting with the third animal, every other one can fly. The rest are plant eaters.

Archie's bush has three red, one orange, five yellow, and six blue flowers.

Liam's bush has four red, three orange, two yellow, and five blue flowers.

Donald's bush has one red, seven orange, and eight yellow flowers.

Dottie's bush has three red, two orange, five yellow, and three blue flowers.

Do all the bushes have an equal number of flowers? _____

What could happen to make the bushes all have an equal number of flowers?

_____

_____

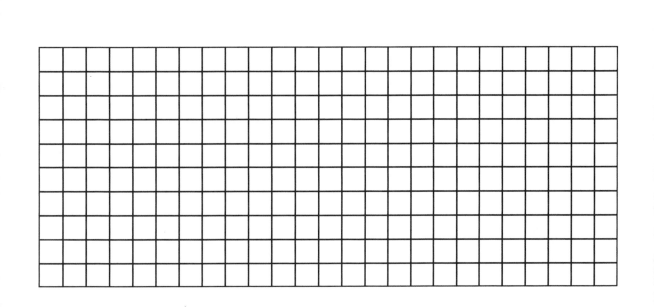

Color six rows of ten blue.

Color seven squares red.

Color another three rows of ten blue.

Color eight squares red.

How many have you colored in?

_____ squares _____ rows of ten

What is that number? _____

Draw a 2" blue square.

Put a 3" yellow triangle to the left of it.

To the right of it put a red circle that is just about as high as the triangle.

Make pictures of these plants, putting those together that go together.

an apple tree
an orange tree
a pine tree
a peach tree
a palm tree
a cactus

Why does each group go together? _____

_____

_____

Write a story to go with this number sentence. Draw a picture to match.
Then provide the answer.

$$20 - 5 = \underline{\quad\quad}$$

_____

_____

_____

_____

_____

_____

_____

There are 24 slices of pizza. How many slices would each person get if there were:

three people? _____

four people? _____

six people? _____

eight people? _____

twelve people? _____

[blank box]

Make pictures of these musical instruments, putting together those that go together.

a tuba
a piano
a violin
a trumpet
a drum
an accordion
a flute
a trombone

Why does each group go together? _____

_____

_____

	red	yellow	blue
Tom			
Marissa			
Hanna			

Tom has three red, four yellow, and four blue marbles. Marissa has eight red and five blue marbles. Hanna has six red, four yellow, and five blue marbles.

Fill in the chart.

What must we do to get an equal number of marbles for everyone?

_____

_____

_____

_____

_____

Mice weigh one pound. Cats weigh ten pounds.

Cats and mice are playing on the seesaw.
On one side are fifteen mice and two cats. On the other
side are three cats and four mice.

Draw the seesaw as it would look that way.

Explain two ways to make the seesaw balance.

_____

_____

_____

_____

_____

Draw three thermometers, each showing different degrees of temperature:

1. When it is too hot.

2. When it is too cold.

3. When it is comfortable.

Draw the following pictures, putting together the things that go together.

a canoe
a train
a helicopter
a bicycle
a truck
a sailboat

Why does each group go together?

_____

_____

How are all these things alike?

_____

Write a story to go with this number sentence. Make a picture
to match. Then provide the answer.

$$50 - 10 = \underline{\hspace{1cm}}$$

_____

_____

_____

_____

_____

_____

Divide the drawing box in half.

In the first half make a picture of something you can do in five minutes.

In the other half make a picture of something that you can do in about an hour.

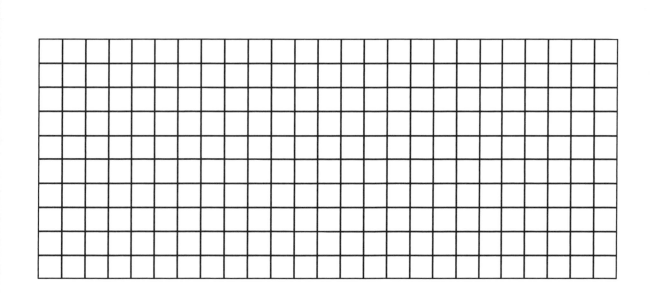

Color eight columns of ten blue.
Color three squares red.

You have _____ squares colored in.

How many squares would you have to take away to have 60 squares colored in?

_____ tens

_____ ones

Paolo had 17 fish. James had 16 fish. Paolo gave 6 fish to Anandi. James gave 8 fish to Anandi.

How many will each have now?

Paolo ____

James ____

Anandi ____

Anandi buys 12 fish and gives half to Paolo and half to James.

Now how many are in each tank? ____

What would we need to do to get an equal number of fish in all three tanks?

_____

The boys have each built a wall. Adam has six red, four yellow, and two blue blocks. Carter has five red, seven yellow, and five blue blocks. Eduardo has nine red, five yellow, and four blue blocks. Nero has five red and eight blue blocks.

Make a chart to show this.

What can we do to make the walls equal?

_____

_____

_____

_____

Some children in our class are making a garden.

Each one has two rows of vegetables.

Three boys and four girls have planted vegetables.

How many rows are there? _____

If we divide the garden in half, how many rows will there
be? _____

┌───┐
│   │
│   │
│   │
│   │
│   │
│   │
│   │
│   │
│   │
└───┘

Trucks cost $1.00. Kites cost 10¢. Marbles cost 1¢.

Elizabeth bought 2 trucks, 5 kites, and 8 marbles.
Glen bought 1 truck, 10 kites, and 12 marbles.
Hester bought 3 trucks, 15 kites, and 20 marbles.

How much did each one spend?

Elizabeth _____

Glen _____

Hester _____

There are 28 blocks in Mack's wall.
There are 32 blocks in Terry's wall.
Draw a picture of the two walls.
How many more blocks does Terry have? _____

Write what you have to do to find out how many blocks were
used in all.

_____

_____

_____

_____

_____

Divide the drawing box in half.

Draw an analog clock and a digital clock in each half.

In the left-hand side, on both clocks, show what time you get up for school.

In the right-hand side, on both clocks, show what time you have dinner.

Hector has 11 marbles. Meg has 6 marbles, Paco has 7, and Edith has 8.

How many marbles are there? _____

If you divided them evenly, how many marbles would each person get? _____

Draw a rectangle 2" high and 3" long.
Measure around it with your centimeter ruler.

About how many centimeters around is it? _____

Five children each brought eight kites to the playground.

How many kites in all? _____

Five other children have no kites.

If we divide all the kites equally among all the children,

how many kites will each one get? _____

Write a story to go with this number sentence.

Make a drawing to match. Then provide the answer.

$$\underline{\hspace{1.5cm}} - 51 = 84$$

_____

_____

_____

_____

_____

_____

On Saturday Manuel gets up at 7:30, eats lunch at 12:00, and goes to bed at 9:15.

Draw three clocks showing the time for each activity.

How much time is there between getting up and eating lunch?

_____ hours _____ minutes

How much time is there between eating lunch and going to bed?

_____ hours _____ minutes

How much time is there between getting up and going to bed?

_____ hours _____ minutes

Carla has six red blocks and four blue blocks.

Dmitri has two fewer red blocks and one more blue block
than Carla has.

Yvonne has one more red block and three fewer blue blocks
than Dmitri has.

How many red blocks in all? _____

How many blue blocks in all? _____

Who has the most red blocks? _____

Who has the fewest blue blocks? _____

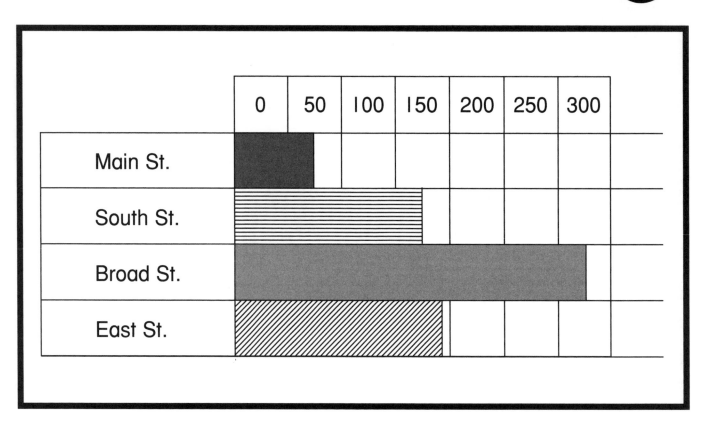

About how many people live on:

Main St.? _____

South St.? _____

Broad St.? _____

East St.? _____

About how many more people are there on Broad St.

than on East St.? _____

About how many fewer people live on Main St. than

live on South St.? _____

Jack is one foot tall.

Xavier is twice as tall as Jack.

Max is twice as tall as Xavier and Jack together.

Josh is twice as tall as Xavier.

Who is probably the best basketball player? _____

Who is probably the youngest? _____

Who is probably the least rapid runner? _____

Make a rectangle that is 2" wide and 5" tall.

Inside the rectangle put a square that is 1" wide.

Simone has four quarters and five dimes.

Tyrone has six quarters and four nickels.

Marilyn has one quarter, ten dimes, and three pennies.

Show this on a chart and write a word problem to go with it.

_____

_____

_____

_____

Draw a shape with six angles.

Divide it in half.

Color $\frac{1}{2}$ red and $\frac{1}{2}$ blue.

The triplets each have five balloons.

Jake has six more balloons than the triplets have.

Tom has four fewer balloons than Jake has.

Kit has one more than Tom has.

Walter has five fewer than Kit has.

How many balloons in all? _____

Draw a triangle that is 3" wide at the base and 4" high.

Inside the triangle draw a line segment that is 2" long.

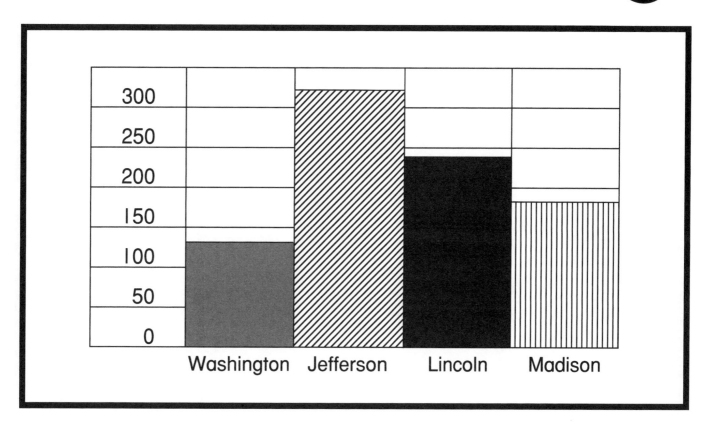

About how many students in each school?

Washington _____

Jefferson _____

Lincoln _____

Madison _____

About how many more students in Jefferson

than in Lincoln? _____

About how many fewer students in Washington

than in Madison? _____

Divide the drawing box into quarters.
You are going to make pictures of 16 things that might be found in school.

You will have the same number of objects in each section of the drawing box.

To make your pictures you will use these shapes in each group:

    Group 1 - circles

    Group 2 - squares

    Group 3 - rectangles

    Group 4 - triangles

How many triangles will you draw? _____

Draw a shape that has five angles.

Divide it into triangles.

Divide the drawing box in half.

In the first half, make a picture of something that might be measured in feet.

In the second half, make a picture of something that might be measured in miles.

	Bruce	Maria	Ted
dollars			
dimes			
pennies			

Fill in the chart and write a story to go with it.

_____

_____

_____

_____

_____

_____

_____

_____

```
┌─────────────────────────────────────────┐
│                                           │
│                                           │
│                                           │
│                                           │
│                                           │
│                                           │
│                                           │
│                                           │
│                                           │
│                                           │
└─────────────────────────────────────────┘
```

The children are having a tug of war.

For the blue team, Betsy weighs 60 pounds, Hiro weighs 90 pounds, Gloria weighs 80 pounds, and Sanjay weighs 60 pounds.

For the red team, Kevin weighs 90 pounds, Lawrence weighs 50 pounds, Serena weighs 70 pounds, and Jana weighs 60 pounds.

Which team has the advantage? _____

How can we make the teams equal? _____

_____

_____

_____

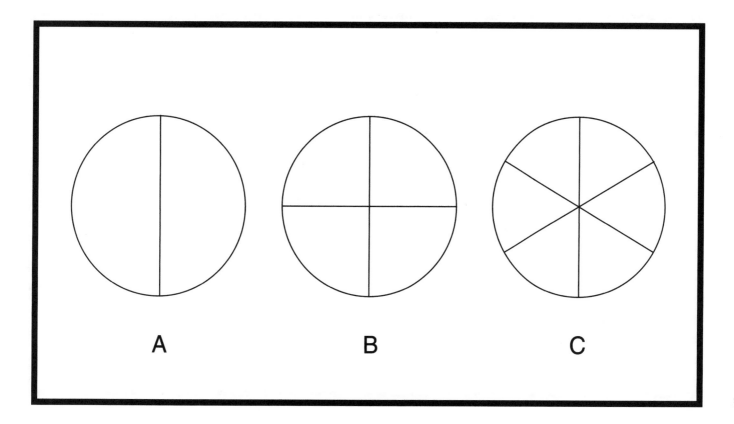

A. Color the left half red and the right half blue.

B. Color $\frac{1}{4}$ yellow, $\frac{1}{4}$ orange, and $\frac{1}{2}$ green.

C. Color $\frac{1}{6}$ red, $\frac{2}{6}$ blue, and $\frac{1}{2}$ yellow.

Make a red shape that is about twice as big as the shaded area.

Make a blue shape that is about three times as big as the shaded area.

Make a green shape that is about the size of the shaded area and the red shape put together.

Write a story to go with this number sentence.

Make a drawing to match. Then provide the answer.

$$42 + \rule{2cm}{0.4pt} = 67$$

_____

_____

_____

_____

_____

_____

_____

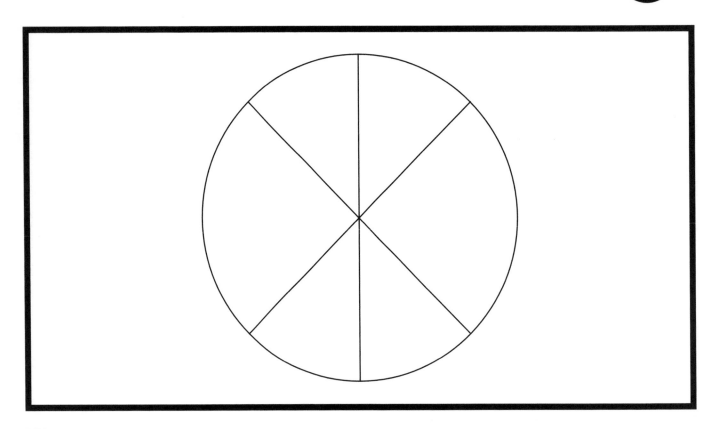

Write a story to go with this graph, and color the graph to
match your story.

_____

_____

_____

_____

_____

_____

_____

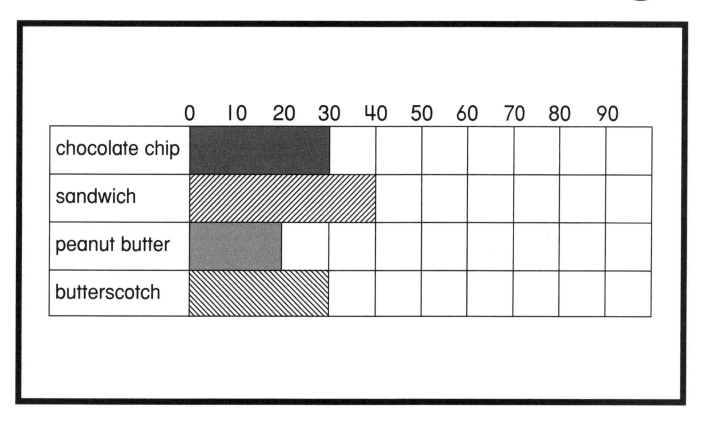

About how many of each kind of cookie are there?

chocolate chip _____

sandwich _____

peanut butter _____

butterscotch _____

About how many more butterscotch cookies are there than

peanut butter? _____

About how many fewer chocolate chip cookies are there than

sandwich? _____

Divide the drawing box in half. Make pictures of things you
would measure using:

1. meters

2. kilometers

_____

Here are ten plants.

There are five flowers on each plant. Two of the flowers are red, and three are yellow.

There are

_____ red flowers.

_____ yellow flowers.

_____ flowers in all.

How many more plants would we need to get 100 flowers? _____

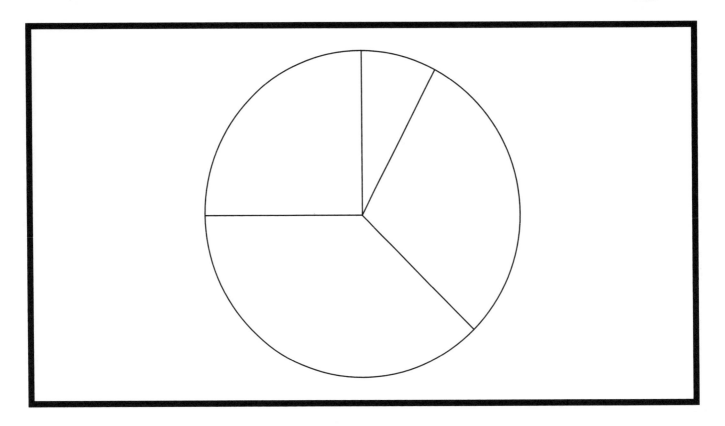

Write a story to go with this graph, and color the graph to
match your story.

_____

_____

_____

_____

_____

_____

_____

Mice weigh one pound. Cats weigh ten pounds. Dogs weigh one hundred pounds.

The animals are playing on the seesaw.

On one side are four dogs, two cats, and one mouse.
On the other side are two dogs, eight cats, and seven mice.

Draw the seesaw with the animals on each side.

What can the animals do to make the seesaw balance?

_____

_____

_____

_____

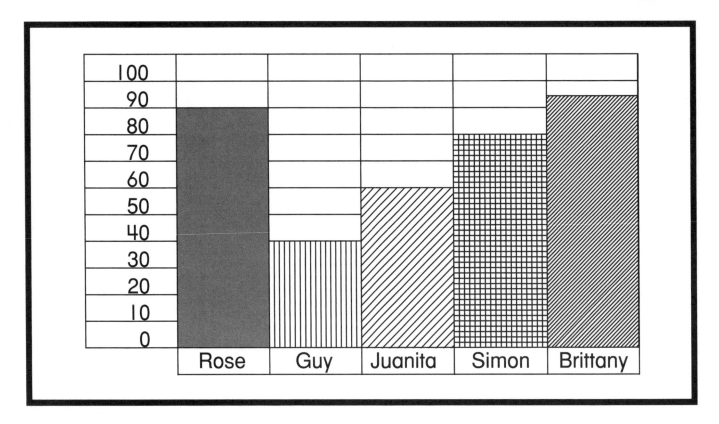

This chart shows cookie sales by five students.

About how many cookies has each person sold?

Rose _____

Guy _____

Juanita _____

Simon _____

Brittany _____

About how many more cookies than Guy has Brittany sold?

_____

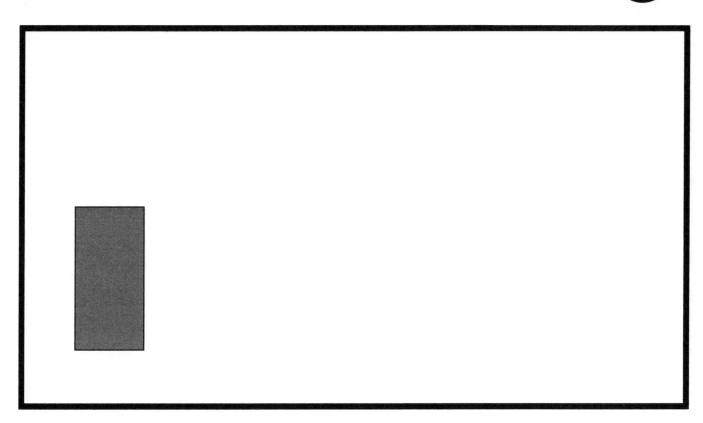

Make a picture of a blue square that is about the same height as the shaded rectangle.

Make a picture of a purple rectangle that is about twice the size as the shaded rectangle.

Write a story about animals to go with this number sentence.
Draw a picture to match. Then provide the answer.

$$5 \times 6 = \_\_\_\_$$

_____

_____

_____

_____

_____

_____

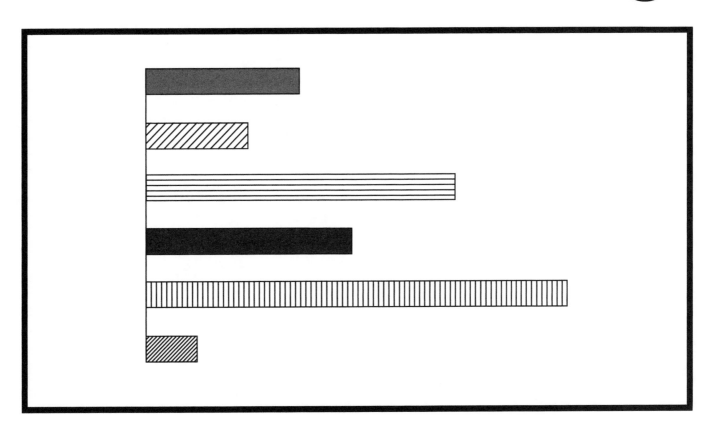

Write a story to go with this graph, using the words MORE, LESS, MOST, and LEAST. Your story should have six characters.

Label the parts of the graph with pictures of each story character.

_____

_____

_____

_____

_____

Eight squirrels each carry four acorns.

How many acorns? _____

They want to store fifty acorns. How many more acorns do

they need? _____

How many squirrels, each carrying four acorns, do they

need? _____

(blank box)

Write a story to go with this number sentence.

Draw a picture to match. Then provide the answer.

$$50 - \underline{} = 34$$

_____

_____

_____

_____

_____

_____

	Dollars	Dimes	Pennies
Gail			
José			
Marcia			
Lu-hong			

Fill in the graph and write a story to go with it.

_____

_____

_____

_____

_____

_____

_____

On the table are eight boxes of crayons. There are ten crayons in each box.

How many crayons are on the table? ____

Sam took two crayons out of each box.

Betty took three crayons out of each box.

How many crayons are left? ____

Make a shape with six angles.

Make as many triangles as you can inside that shape.

Make a rectangle 3 cm high and 4 cm long.

Inside the rectangle create three triangles.

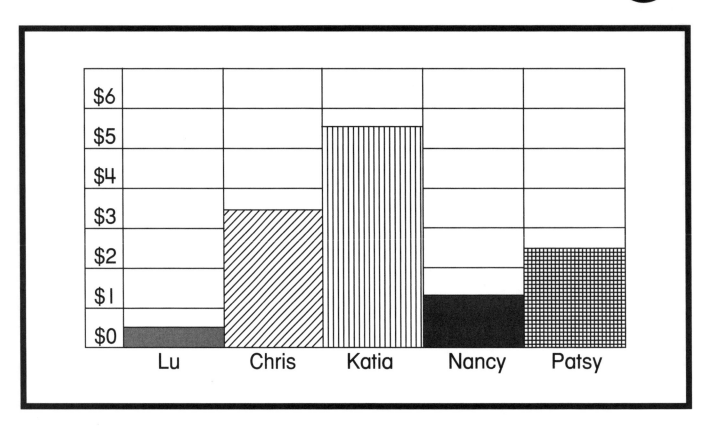

About how much money does each person have?

Lu _____

Chris _____

Katia _____

Nancy _____

Patsy _____

About how much more money than Nancy does Patsy have? _____

About how much less money than Chris does Lu have? _____

Name _____

We are going to use paper clips for measuring. Each student will get 5 clips. There are 28 students in the class. There are 50 clips in each box.

How many boxes will we need? _____

Will there be clips left over? _____

How many? _____

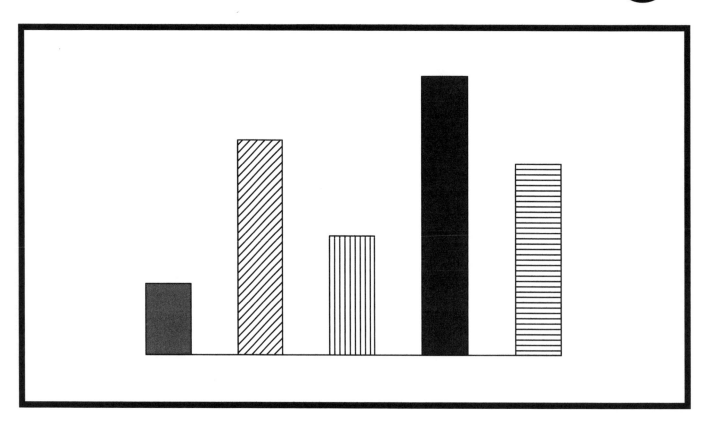

Write a story to go with this graph, using the words MORE,
LESS, MOST, and LEAST. Then label the graph with words
or pictures.

_____

_____

_____

_____

_____

_____

Write a story to go with this number sentence.

Draw a picture to match. Then provide the answer.

$$76 - \underline{\hspace{1cm}} = 54$$

_____

_____

_____

_____

_____

_____

_____

Divide the drawing box in half. On one side, make a picture
of something that could be measured in inches. On the other
side, make a picture of something that could be measured
in yards.

[blank box]

We went on a bird walk. We counted 25 robins, 32 blue jays, 19 cardinals, 4 eagles, 2 hummingbirds, and 1 owl.

Make a chart that shows this.

How many more cardinals are there than owls? _____

How many more robins are there than hummingbirds? _____

How many fewer eagles are there than blue jays? _____

Mice weigh one pound, cats weigh ten pounds, and dogs weigh one hundred pounds.

The animals are playing on the seesaw.
On one side are two dogs, four cats, and eight mice.
On the other side is a baby elephant that weighs 316 pounds.

Draw the seesaw as it would look with all the animals.

Write about two ways to make the seesaw balance.

_____

_____

_____

_____

There are 12 people on each gymnastics team. Each person holds 4 flags.

How many flags will one team have? _____

There are three teams in the gymnasium.

How many people are in the gymnasium? _____

How many flags are there? _____

Draw a circle that is 5 cm across.

Put a line segment inside the circle that is 3 cm long.

Which shape can most easily be divided into two equal parts?

Guess before you make the picture. _____

    I. a shape with three angles

    2. a shape with four angles

    3. a shape with five angles

Betsy has three red, two blue, and four yellow dresses.
Sunita has one orange, three green, and two purple dresses.
Wendy has two orange, one red, one purple, and one yellow
dress.

How many dresses does each one have?

Betsy _____

Sunita _____

Wendy _____

How many dresses of each color are there?

red _____   green _____

orange _____   blue _____

yellow _____   purple _____

Write a story to go with this number sentence.

Draw a picture to match. Then provide the answer.

_____ + 65 = 93

_____

_____

_____

_____

_____

_____

[Blank box for drawing]

We have 24 students divided into 6 equal groups. They are sitting at tables painting.

Each table has one yellow paint jar, twice as many red jars, and twice as many blue jars as red ones.

How many students are in each group? _____

How many blue jars are on each table? _____

How many red jars in all? _____

How many paint jars in all? _____

Create a design with three squares, five rectangles,
five circles, and three triangles.

Make the design symmetrical.

We have 40 pencils to be divided equally among Bob, Damian, Carlos, George, and Howard.

How many pencils will each get?

Write a sentence that tells what you had to do to get the answer.

_____

_____

_____

_____

Draw two pictures.

The first picture should show something that can be measured in centimeters.

The second picture should show something that can be measured in kilometers.

	Antonio	Carla	Edward	Gigi	Hwan
$1.00					
90¢					
80¢					
70¢					
60¢					
50¢					
40¢					
30¢					
20¢					
10¢					
0¢					

Antonio has 76¢, Carla has 31¢, Edward has 18¢, Gigi has 87¢, and Hwan has 68¢.

Fill in the chart.

At the toy store, yo-yos cost 12¢, tops cost 25¢, balls cost 15¢, and trucks cost 45¢.

Soon-Li wants to know how many of each she can buy.

What else does she need to know?

_____

Make up a problem. Write about it below.
Then draw a picture to go with the problem.

_____

_____

_____

Make pictures of two analog clocks. Put in all the numbers
on both clocks.

Divide the first clock into halves.

Color the left half red and the right half blue.

Divide the second clock into quarters.

Color each quarter a different color.

There are 12 pencils in each box. There are 8 boxes on the table.

How many pencils are on the table? _____

There are 24 students in the class.

If we divide the pencils evenly, how many will each one

get? _____

	0	$1	$2	$3	$4	$5	$6	$7	$8	$9	$10
Brad											
Chet											
Frank											
Harris											
Juan											

Brad earned $2.50.

Chet earned twice as much as Brad earned.

Frank earned $1.00 more than Chet earned.

Harris earned $1.00 less than Brad earned.

Juan earned twice as much as Harris earned.

Fill in the chart.

Make pictures of two analog clocks. Fill in all the numbers on both clocks.

On the first clock, show the time as 9:50.

On the second clock, show the time as 40 minutes earlier.

	Li	James	Violet	Teresa
quarters				
dimes				
nickels				
pennies				

Li has $1.02.

James has 83¢.

Violet has 80¢.

Teresa has $1.06.

Fill in the chart.

About how much more money than Violet does Li have? _____

Using stars, make a picture to go with this number sentence.
Then provide the answer.

$$5 \times 6 = \underline{\quad\quad}$$

Draw a rectangle that is twice as high and half as long as the rectangle shown.

Nov.		
Dec.		
Jan.		
Feb.		

Write a story that tells how much snow fell in each winter month, and how many snowmen you could make.

_____

_____

_____

_____

_____

_____

Fill in the chart, using pictures at the top to show which column is for snow and which is for snowmen.

Jennifer is going to buy fruit. She has $3.00.

She sees apples, cherries, oranges, and watermelons.

What does she need to know in order to make her purchases?

_____

_____

Make up a problem and write it below. Then draw what
Jennifer buys.

_____

_____

_____

June has 30 days. Draw a calendar for June, and put the last day on a Thursday.

The 14th was supposed to be the last day of school, but we had to add six days to make up for all the bad weather days in the winter.

Put a red circle around the last day of school.

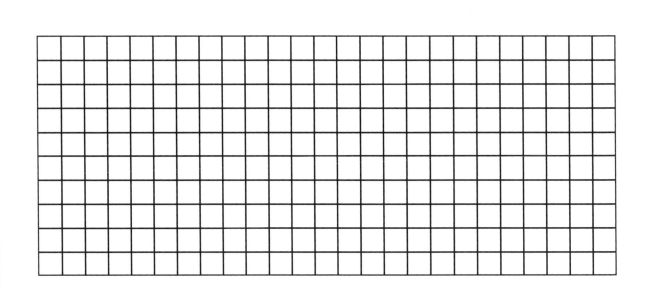

Fill in the grid above to show this problem. Then write your answer in the space provided.

$$80 \div 10 = \underline{\qquad}$$

READ IT! DRAW IT! SOLVE IT! • GRADE 3

Copyright© Dale Seymour Publications®

April has 30 days. Make a calendar for April, and put the
last day on Tuesday.

We have a science fair on the 10th, a concert on the 18th,
and a field trip on the 25th.

How many days are there between the science fair and the

concert? _____

How many school days are there between the science fair

and the field trip? _____

Draw two lines: one approximately 2" long, and one about 4" long.

Divide the shorter line into four equal parts.

Divide the longer line into six equal parts.

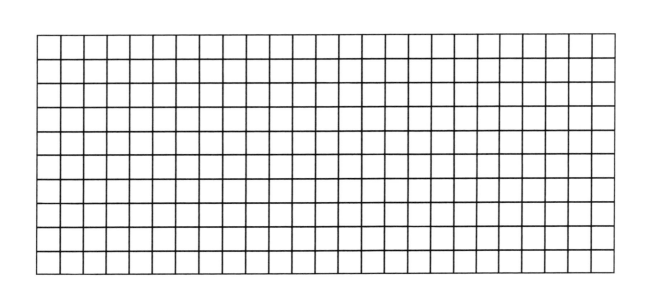

Fill in the grid above to show this problem. Then write your answer.

$$10 \times 6 = \underline{\hspace{1cm}}$$

	0	10	20	30	40	50	60	70	80	90	100
Ivan											
Krista											
Luigi											
Nicholas											
Quentin											

Ivan has 50¢.

Krista has $\frac{1}{2}$ of that.

Luigi has 10¢ more than Krista.

Nicholas has twice as much as Luigi.

Quentin has 30¢ less than Nicholas.

Fill in the graph above to show how much money each person has.

A football field is 100 yards long. Draw a football field, putting in the end zones and all the yard lines.

Draw a football field. Sam punted the ball from his own
20-yard line to the other team's 35-yard line. Matt caught
the ball and ran it back to Sam's 30-yard line. Draw this
on your field, using a dotted line for a kick, and a straight
line for a run.

kick ·············

run _____

Draw a football field, and show what happened.

-------------- pass

· · · · · · · · · · · · · kick

——————— run

Ben kicked the ball from his 35-yard line, and Melvin caught it on his 45-yard line. He was tackled there.

On the next play, Hector passed the ball from the 45-yard line. Melvin caught it on the 50-yard line and ran with it to the 20-yard line.

	quarters	dimes	nickels	pennies
Barbara				
Sangeeta				
Jane				

Fill in the chart and write a word problem to go with it.

_____

_____

_____

_____

_____

September has 30 days. Make a calendar for September, and have the first day be a Thursday.

Your teacher gives you an assignment on September 5 and tells you to hand it in in exactly two weeks.

You will hand in the assignment on _____.

	Mon.	Tues.	Wed.	Thurs.	Fri.	Sat.	Sun.
Mara							
Tyrell							
Gloria							
Betsy							
Hiro							

Fill in the chart and write a story to go with it.

_____

_____

_____

_____

_____

_____

_____

_____

Shawn has a tree in his yard that is quite small.

Draw your own tree that is about twice as wide and three times as tall.

Baseball Cards

	10	20	30	40	50	60	70	80
Lynn								
Olive								
Gabor								
Rachel								

Lynn has 54 cards.

Olive has 28 cards.

Gabor has 61 cards.

Rachel has 73 cards.

Fill in the grid as accurately as you can.

We are learning a new language.

One is written like this: /

Five looks like this: ▱

Ten looks like this: ▱ ▱

What do you think the rest of the numbers between one and twenty would look like? Draw a picture of each number above, being sure to label each one.

Sylvia has five containers.

The red one holds one cup.

The orange one holds twice as much as the red one.

The yellow one holds twice as much as the orange one.

The green one holds as much as the orange and yellow ones together.

The blue one holds half as much as the green one.

Draw a picture of each container.

Gold Stars

50				
40				
30				
20				
10				
0				
	Olive	Sasha	Tammy	Victoria

Olive has 22 gold stars.

Sasha has 38.

Tammy has 15.

Victoria has 41.

Fill in the grid as accurately as you can.

Show the directions north, south, east, and west in the drawing box.

Draw a picture of Main Street.

Make a picture of Mary's house about one inch long and two inches wide, facing north.

Make a picture of Virgil's house, twice as long and half as wide as Mary's house, facing south.

	red team	orange team	yellow team	blue team
girls	2	5	1	7
boys	3	3	5	0

Which team has the most people? _____

Which team has the fewest people? _____

How many girls are there? _____

How many boys are there? _____

How many players in all? _____

How many people on the red team? _____

How many people on the orange team? _____

How many people on the yellow team? _____

How many people on the blue team? _____

Write a word problem in which you have to divide numbers
of people by how many can fit in each helicopter. Then draw
a picture of your word problem.

_____

_____

_____

_____

Juan has five containers.

The red one holds eight cups.

The orange one holds half as much as the red one.

The yellow one holds half as much as the orange one.

The green one holds as much as the yellow and orange ones together.

The blue one holds half as much as the green one.

Draw a picture of each container.

	red	orange	yellow	green
Sanjay				
Bill				
Hiro				
Pete				
Richard				

Fill in the graph. Give each student the same number of marbles in all, but give them different numbers of each of the colors.

Name ___

DAY 177

Write a word problem about children and marbles, using multiplication. Then draw a picture of your word problem.

READ IT! DRAW IT SOLVE IT! • GRADE 3

177

100					
90					
80					
70					
60					
50					
40					
30					
20					
10					
0					
	Susan	Aya	Lourdes	Josh	Paul

Show the students' grades on this graph as accurately as you can.

Susan got an 84.

Aya got a 99.

Lourdes got a 63.

Josh got a 76.

Paul got a 71.

Jan.					
Feb.					
March					
April					
May					
June					
	1	2	3	4	5

Make up a story to go with this graph. Then fill in the graph.

_____

_____

_____

_____

_____

_____

_____

_____

35			
30			
25			
20			
15			
10			
5			
0			

Make up a story that has three characters and that uses one number from 0 to 35 for each character. Then label the columns and fill in the graph.

_____

_____

_____

_____

_____